THE MORNING MAGIC 5-MINUTE JOURNAL

TANYA J. PETERSON, MS, NCC

THE MORNING MAGIC 5-MINUTE JOURNAL

INSPIRING PROMPTS TO
SET INTENTIONS & LIVE
WITH GRATITUDE ALL DAY

ROCKRIDGE
PRESS

Interior and Cover Designer: Rachel Haeseker
Art Producer: Tom Hood
Editor: Rochelle Torke
Production Editor: Andrew Yackira

ISBN: Print 978-1-64739-919-1

R0

TO MY GRADUATE PROFESSORS AT
SOUTH DAKOTA STATE, FOR ALLOWING
ME TO FOCUS ON POSITIVE PSYCHOLOGY
BEFORE IT WAS THE POPULAR COUNSELING
APPROACH IT IS TODAY.

THIS JOURNAL
BELONGS TO

INTRODUCTION

Greetings, and great day to you! Welcome to your morning magic journal. Even better, welcome to your brand-new day. By beginning a morning journaling practice and picking up this book, you've already completed an important step toward creating quality days. You know quite a bit about what you want for yourself and your life, and this journal will help you hone it, own it, and make it happen.

I'm so pleased you've chosen this journal, because I firmly believe it can have a powerful impact on your mornings, your days, and your life. I've written this with the express intention of helping you shape and build your positive momentum, preparing yourself for whatever the day holds.

I've found in my own personal life, and in helping others, that journaling is a powerful way for us to create the life we want to live. Life can be rough at times. I've faced a variety of obstacles including anxiety, a traumatic brain injury, and relationship struggles. I've also recently been diagnosed with several chronic health issues (multiple autoimmune and digestive disorders). These snags are part of my life, but they don't define my life. I realized long ago that while I can't choose everything that happens to me, I can choose my focus and response. I decided I wanted to thrive in my life no matter what obstacles appear in my path.

That decision is what initially led me to journaling. Getting my thoughts, emotions, and ideas out of my head and out in front of me put me in charge of myself and my life. Reflecting on what truly mattered to me helped me appreciate all the wonderful things already in my life, to intentionally choose my attitude, and to further define the direction I wanted to go. As I worked with people in a teaching and counseling relationship, I began to suggest journaling as a way of living life fully and purposefully. Many people have told me that journaling has been a transformative and sustaining practice for them, too, which is why I create journals like this one. I want people to have this tool available to enhance the quality of their lives. I want you to have a positive, helpful way to live each day fully, with intention, purpose, gratitude, and meaning.

The book you are holding is your own. Create your unique experience with it. I encourage you to use it in the morning, but don't feel like you must use it every morning. Journaling regularly is effective because frequent practice is what creates long-term perspectives and habits. "Regular," though, doesn't necessarily mean daily. Even a few times a week is enough to cultivate a deep sense of peace, purpose, and gratitude so you can bring your best self to the world and build a satisfying life full of joy.

Starting your day on a positive, grateful note can help you stay focused and live in each moment rather than stuck in your mind. Create and own the rich life you deserve!

"The first hour of the morning is the rudder of the day."

–HENRY WARD BEECHER

YOUR BEST DAY STARTS HERE

Sometimes, just as we're waking up, a wave of thoughts rush to mind before we've even opened our eyes. How you react to these thoughts and emotions is an important choice in setting the tone for your day. By taking a few minutes in the morning for mindful journaling, you can organize your thoughts, cultivate gratitude, and set an intention around how you'd like to think, feel, and act that day. You empower yourself to sail around and through any obstacle with grace and effectiveness.

Positive journaling that includes gratitude isn't just trendy fluff. Researchers in many fields, including mindfulness and positive psychology, have been studying the effects of regular and intentional mindful journaling, and the results are encouraging.

* Journaling just twice a week to reflect on people and situations for which you're grateful can improve symptoms of work-related stress and depression, according to a 2015 study published in the *Journal of Consulting and Clinical Psychology*.
* Creating a regular practice of intentional journaling that includes gratitude increases our ability to cope with stress and helps us see the positives in our lives that tend to get lost in problems and negativity, as attested by a National Institute of Health's *NIH News in Health* report.
* Participants in a 2003 study who recorded thoughts of gratitude experienced enhanced well-being and benefits in their social lives. The study was conducted in part by Richard Emmons, a prominent researcher in positive psychology and gratitude.
* A 2016 study, published in the journal *Psychotherapy Research*, demonstrated that people in counseling for various mental health conditions who included at-home journal writing as part of their therapy had better outcomes than those who either completed expressive writing exercises or did no writing exercises.

These are only a handful of research examples that show the numerous benefits of regular journaling on mental health and well-being. While each person's experience with journaling is unique and highly personal, starting your day with this journal can impact how you feel and how you respond to stressors all day long. Take heart knowing that this doesn't require a huge chunk of your time. I've developed this journal to be a quick and joyful way to begin a new day. With just five minutes of journaling, you'll notice a difference in your sense of contentment and inner peace. You may come to savor these minutes so much that you'd hardly let a morning slip by without turning to your journal.

HOW TO RELISH THIS JOURNAL— AND YOUR DAY

As you flip through your journal, you'll see that the bulk of it consists of Daily Journal Pages. These simple prompts will help you develop an intentional mindset. The way you think becomes a habit, a default pattern of thinking that shapes the way you approach the world and your role in it.

We humans have a negativity bias. We're hardwired to look for and zoom in on the bad, the dangerous, the stuff that keeps us mired in muck. Why do we do this? In the earliest days of human existence, life was all about survival. If someone wasn't on high alert for the bad, their chances of survival diminished. This happens even in modern times. From infancy, babies must be on alert for the bad in order to receive the good. In your early days, you wouldn't have been fed, given a fresh diaper, or received a nurturing hug if you didn't know that something was wrong (you were hungry, wet, or lonely) and alerted your caregivers. So, tuning into the negative helps us survive. It doesn't, however, help us thrive and be happy. To do so, we must try to seek the positive and turn it into habit. Enter your Daily Journal Pages!

Every morning you journal, you'll have the opportunity to choose your perspective and shape your outlook for the day. The categories will be the same to help you learn to override the negativity bias long-term, but your intentions for each day will change. This way, you can make the most out of every day and all that the day holds for you.

You'll also encounter Inspiration Pages peppered throughout your journal. These are designed to enhance your mindful attention to and gratitude for numerous facets of your overall well-being. They're inspired by the human needs we all share, and move from basic, physical needs to more complex needs such as finding purpose and creating meaning in your life. The Inspiration Pages will help you go deeper and cultivate a rich life experience, day by day and moment by moment.

Here's a snapshot of what you'll encounter in your journal.

DAILY JOURNAL PAGE OVERVIEW

VISION | WHAT WOULD MAKE TODAY GREAT...

Consider your vision for today. How would you like the day to unfold? Capture your ambitions here, however they show up in your mind. Make them as specific as you'd like.

INTENTION | TODAY I WILL...

Record how you will put your vision into action. You can write down big steps you'd like to take, or one simple action that's most important to you now.

GRATITUDE | I'M GRATEFUL FOR...

Reflect on things big, small, or in between for which you are grateful. There is no such thing as a "little" gratitude because every moment of gratitude helps us flex our positivity and awareness.

RELEASE | I LET GO OF...

Commit to letting go of things that aren't serving you. What worries, thoughts, or situations need attention? How will you release them from your mental grasp? Will you take a specific action to solve an ongoing problem? The possibilities for letting go are numerous.

SPACE | ON MY MIND/IN MY HEART/ON MY SHOULDERS/ LIGHTING MY WAY...

Use this open writing space to express anything else that's on your mind. What thoughts flashed across your awareness as you woke up? A desire or inspiration? A worry or concern? When you release something negative, you make room in your mind, heart, and life for something bigger. How will you fill your growing space?

INSPIRATION PAGE OVERVIEW

THEME

Each page features a daily theme, one of the basic human needs, to guide your thoughts and intentions in fresh directions.

TITLE

The focal point for the day's theme.

RELATED QUOTE

Inspiring quotes are energizing and motivating and can help us think in new, positive ways.

REFLECTION

An expanded consideration of today's theme to help you apply it to your own life.

SELF-INQUIRY

Respond to prompts that help you explore and enhance your own thoughts, feelings, and experiences—as you expand your sense of well-being, gratitude, and purpose.

GRATEFUL FOR THE BASICS

FOOD

"One cannot think well, love well, sleep well, if one has not dined well."

—VIRGINIA WOOLF,
A ROOM OF ONE'S OWN

REFLECTION

Food is one of the most fundamental of all human needs. Without it, we wither and die. With healthy food, we flourish. It's easy to take our meals for granted or slip into thinking of cooking as another task on our to-do list. However, whenever good, nourishing food is available to us, it is a cause for celebration. Deepen your positive relationship with your meals. Try pausing mindfully and feeling gratitude for your vital source of life, and celebrate it.

SELF-INQUIRY INVITATIONS

✳ Write about one of the most memorable meals you've ever had. What made it special?
✳ What does good food mean to you? How would you describe your favorite food? Use all your senses: sight, sound, smell, feeling (texture), and taste.
✳ What do your favorite foods do for you? How can you use them to further enrich your life?
✳ Describe your ideal way to eat a meal. Do you enjoy eating alone, mindfully savoring every bite? Do you prefer the company of a loved one, being fully present with them in the experience?

VISION | **WHAT WOULD MAKE TODAY GREAT...**

INTENTION | **TODAY I WILL...**

GRATITUDE | **I'M GRATEFUL FOR...**

RELEASE | **I LET GO OF...**

SPACE | **ON MY MIND/IN MY HEART/ON MY SHOULDERS/ LIGHTING MY WAY...**

VISION | WHAT WOULD MAKE TODAY GREAT...

_____

_____

INTENTION | TODAY I WILL...

_____

_____

GRATITUDE | I'M GRATEFUL FOR...

_____

_____

RELEASE | I LET GO OF...

_____

_____

SPACE | ON MY MIND/IN MY HEART/ON MY SHOULDERS/
LIGHTING MY WAY...

_____

_____

_____

_____

VISION | WHAT WOULD MAKE TODAY GREAT...

....

....

INTENTION | TODAY I WILL...

....

....

GRATITUDE | I'M GRATEFUL FOR...

....

....

RELEASE | I LET GO OF...

....

....

**SPACE | ON MY MIND/IN MY HEART/ON MY SHOULDERS/
LIGHTING MY WAY...**

....

....

....

....

VISION | **WHAT WOULD MAKE TODAY GREAT...**

INTENTION | **TODAY I WILL...**

GRATITUDE | **I'M GRATEFUL FOR...**

RELEASE | **I LET GO OF...**

SPACE | **ON MY MIND/IN MY HEART/ON MY SHOULDERS/
LIGHTING MY WAY...**

VISION | WHAT WOULD MAKE TODAY GREAT...

....

....

INTENTION | TODAY I WILL...

....

....

GRATITUDE | I'M GRATEFUL FOR...

....

....

RELEASE | I LET GO OF...

....

....

SPACE | ON MY MIND/IN MY HEART/ON MY SHOULDERS/
LIGHTING MY WAY...

....

....

....

....

....

VISION | WHAT WOULD MAKE TODAY GREAT...

INTENTION | TODAY I WILL...

GRATITUDE | I'M GRATEFUL FOR...

RELEASE | I LET GO OF...

SPACE | ON MY MIND/IN MY HEART/ON MY SHOULDERS/
LIGHTING MY WAY...

VISION | **WHAT WOULD MAKE TODAY GREAT...**

INTENTION | **TODAY I WILL...**

GRATITUDE | **I'M GRATEFUL FOR...**

RELEASE | **I LET GO OF...**

SPACE | **ON MY MIND/IN MY HEART/ON MY SHOULDERS/
LIGHTING MY WAY...**

VISION | **WHAT WOULD MAKE TODAY GREAT...**

....

....

INTENTION | **TODAY I WILL...**

....

....

GRATITUDE | **I'M GRATEFUL FOR...**

....

....

RELEASE | **I LET GO OF...**

....

....

SPACE | **ON MY MIND/IN MY HEART/ON MY SHOULDERS/ LIGHTING MY WAY...**

....

....

....

....

GRATEFUL FOR THE BASICS

HOME

"The ache for home lives in all of us. The safe place where we can go as we are and not be questioned."

—MAYA ANGELOU,
*ALL GOD'S CHILDREN NEED
TRAVELING SHOES*

REFLECTION

Home is safety. It's our shelter from the elements and our respite from stresses in the world. Home is comfort and solace, the place where you can relax into yourself and simply be. Home is more than materials, a particular location, or the way the light shines on your favorite chair (though it can be those things, too). Home is an experience, a feeling. Sometimes, you might experience conflicts or problems at home. Rather than getting caught up in what is lacking or imperfect, shift your perspective to the ways your home protects and nurtures you physically and emotionally.

SELF-INQUIRY INVITATIONS

* Express the concept of home as though you were teaching it to a young child.
* What does it mean for you to feel at home? Describe the experience and the feelings that accompany it.
* Describe aspects of your home using all five of your senses (sight, sound, smell, touch, and taste).
* It has been said that home is where your heart is. Why is your heart there? What about your home makes you grateful?

VISION | WHAT WOULD MAKE TODAY GREAT...

INTENTION | TODAY I WILL...

GRATITUDE | I'M GRATEFUL FOR...

RELEASE | I LET GO OF...

SPACE | ON MY MIND/IN MY HEART/ON MY SHOULDERS/
LIGHTING MY WAY...

VISION | WHAT WOULD MAKE TODAY GREAT...

INTENTION | TODAY I WILL...

GRATITUDE | I'M GRATEFUL FOR...

RELEASE | I LET GO OF...

SPACE | ON MY MIND/IN MY HEART/ON MY SHOULDERS/
LIGHTING MY WAY...

VISION | **WHAT WOULD MAKE TODAY GREAT...**

INTENTION | **TODAY I WILL...**

GRATITUDE | **I'M GRATEFUL FOR...**

RELEASE | **I LET GO OF...**

SPACE | **ON MY MIND/IN MY HEART/ON MY SHOULDERS/
LIGHTING MY WAY...**

VISION | **WHAT WOULD MAKE TODAY GREAT...**

INTENTION | **TODAY I WILL...**

GRATITUDE | **I'M GRATEFUL FOR...**

RELEASE | **I LET GO OF...**

SPACE | **ON MY MIND/IN MY HEART/ON MY SHOULDERS/
LIGHTING MY WAY...**

VISION | WHAT WOULD MAKE TODAY GREAT...

INTENTION | TODAY I WILL...

GRATITUDE | I'M GRATEFUL FOR...

RELEASE | I LET GO OF...

SPACE | ON MY MIND/IN MY HEART/ON MY SHOULDERS/
LIGHTING MY WAY...

VISION | **WHAT WOULD MAKE TODAY GREAT...**

....

....

INTENTION | **TODAY I WILL...**

....

....

GRATITUDE | **I'M GRATEFUL FOR...**

....

....

RELEASE | **I LET GO OF...**

....

....

SPACE | **ON MY MIND/IN MY HEART/ON MY SHOULDERS/
LIGHTING MY WAY...**

....

....

....

....

....

VISION | **WHAT WOULD MAKE TODAY GREAT...**

INTENTION | **TODAY I WILL...**

GRATITUDE | **I'M GRATEFUL FOR...**

RELEASE | **I LET GO OF...**

SPACE | **ON MY MIND/IN MY HEART/ON MY SHOULDERS/ LIGHTING MY WAY...**

VISION | **WHAT WOULD MAKE TODAY GREAT...**

INTENTION | **TODAY I WILL...**

GRATITUDE | **I'M GRATEFUL FOR...**

RELEASE | **I LET GO OF...**

SPACE | **ON MY MIND/IN MY HEART/ON MY SHOULDERS/
LIGHTING MY WAY...**

GRATEFUL FOR THE BASICS

HEALTH

"Look to your health . . . [It is] a blessing that money cannot buy."

–IZAAK WALTON,
THE COMPLETE ANGLER

REFLECTION

There are many ways to define health. Health and wellness are so much more than the absence of disease. Even when you are experiencing a serious illness, you have health in other ways. Likewise, days arrive when we don't feel our best, when our bodies don't shine with the vitality we would call ideal. Sometimes we know why and sometimes we don't. On these days, we have the opportunity to practice both self-inquiry and hope. We can observe our thoughts and recent choices, looking for the actions that might lead us back to our more vital self. Happily, many aspects of your health are largely in your control, and you can increase your well-being starting now. Health encompasses energy, vitality, balanced mood, confidence, and the ability to show up for the moments of your life.

SELF-INQUIRY INVITATIONS:

* What does "good health" mean to you? Think of what it means for you to feel healthy, "do" healthy, and be healthy overall.
* How can you add nutritious foods into your daily diet? Make a list of small changes you can make today.
* Habits form the foundation of health. What is one unhealthy action you can eliminate today? What healthy action will you replace it with?
* What is one positive change you will notice in your life as your health increases?

VISION | WHAT WOULD MAKE TODAY GREAT...

....

....

INTENTION | TODAY I WILL...

....

....

GRATITUDE | I'M GRATEFUL FOR...

....

....

RELEASE | I LET GO OF...

....

....

SPACE | ON MY MIND/IN MY HEART/ON MY SHOULDERS/
LIGHTING MY WAY...

....

....

....

....

....

VISION | **WHAT WOULD MAKE TODAY GREAT...**

INTENTION | **TODAY I WILL...**

GRATITUDE | **I'M GRATEFUL FOR...**

RELEASE | **I LET GO OF...**

SPACE | **ON MY MIND/IN MY HEART/ON MY SHOULDERS/
LIGHTING MY WAY...**

VISION | **WHAT WOULD MAKE TODAY GREAT...**

....

....

INTENTION | **TODAY I WILL...**

....

....

GRATITUDE | **I'M GRATEFUL FOR...**

....

....

RELEASE | **I LET GO OF...**

....

....

SPACE | **ON MY MIND/IN MY HEART/ON MY SHOULDERS/
LIGHTING MY WAY...**

....

....

....

....

....

VISION | WHAT WOULD MAKE TODAY GREAT...

INTENTION | TODAY I WILL...

GRATITUDE | I'M GRATEFUL FOR...

RELEASE | I LET GO OF...

SPACE | ON MY MIND/IN MY HEART/ON MY SHOULDERS/
LIGHTING MY WAY...

VISION | **WHAT WOULD MAKE TODAY GREAT...**

....

....

INTENTION | **TODAY I WILL...**

....

....

GRATITUDE | **I'M GRATEFUL FOR...**

....

....

RELEASE | **I LET GO OF...**

....

....

SPACE | **ON MY MIND/IN MY HEART/ON MY SHOULDERS/ LIGHTING MY WAY...**

....

....

....

....

VISION | WHAT WOULD MAKE TODAY GREAT...

INTENTION | TODAY I WILL...

GRATITUDE | I'M GRATEFUL FOR...

RELEASE | I LET GO OF...

SPACE | ON MY MIND/IN MY HEART/ON MY SHOULDERS/
LIGHTING MY WAY...

VISION | **WHAT WOULD MAKE TODAY GREAT...**

INTENTION | **TODAY I WILL...**

GRATITUDE | **I'M GRATEFUL FOR...**

RELEASE | **I LET GO OF...**

SPACE | **ON MY MIND/IN MY HEART/ON MY SHOULDERS/ LIGHTING MY WAY...**

VISION | **WHAT WOULD MAKE TODAY GREAT...**

....

....

INTENTION | **TODAY I WILL...**

....

....

GRATITUDE | **I'M GRATEFUL FOR...**

....

....

RELEASE | **I LET GO OF...**

....

....

SPACE | **ON MY MIND/IN MY HEART/ON MY SHOULDERS/
LIGHTING MY WAY...**

....

....

....

....

GRATEFUL FOR SAFETY

SAFE IN
THE WORLD

"*You gain strength, courage, and confidence by every experience in which you really stop to look fear in the face. You are able to say to yourself, 'I lived through this horror. I can take the next thing that comes along.' ... You must do the thing you think you cannot do.*"

–ELEANOR ROOSEVELT, *YOU LEARN BY LIVING*

REFLECTION

We often take our safety for granted, inadvertently letting our fears grow and hold us back. How safe do you feel in your world? Are you free from violence? Are you free from physical and emotional harm? Do you feel safe to move about? Can you express yourself without being ridiculed or bullied? If any answer is "no," then take immediate measures to secure your safety. If your answers are "yes," then relish your freedom of movement, mind, and self. Celebrate your freedom by boldly facing your fears, knowing that you are safe and secure.

SELF-INQUIRY INVITATIONS

* What does safety mean to you? What circumstances must be in place for you to feel safe?
* Do you have a fear that is holding you back from trying something new or taking a risk? What, specifically, are you afraid might happen if the fear came true?
* Safety isn't a guarantee that we won't run into problems in our lives. What do you do to maintain a sense of safety and security despite your fears or other negative situations?
* What is, in Eleanor Roosevelt's words, one "thing you think you cannot do?" How willing are you to give it a try?

VISION | **WHAT WOULD MAKE TODAY GREAT...**

INTENTION | **TODAY I WILL...**

GRATITUDE | **I'M GRATEFUL FOR...**

RELEASE | **I LET GO OF...**

SPACE | **ON MY MIND/IN MY HEART/ON MY SHOULDERS/ LIGHTING MY WAY...**

VISION | WHAT WOULD MAKE TODAY GREAT...

INTENTION | TODAY I WILL...

GRATITUDE | I'M GRATEFUL FOR...

RELEASE | I LET GO OF...

SPACE | ON MY MIND/IN MY HEART/ON MY SHOULDERS/
LIGHTING MY WAY...

VISION | **WHAT WOULD MAKE TODAY GREAT...**

INTENTION | **TODAY I WILL...**

GRATITUDE | **I'M GRATEFUL FOR...**

RELEASE | **I LET GO OF...**

SPACE | **ON MY MIND/IN MY HEART/ON MY SHOULDERS/
LIGHTING MY WAY...**

VISION | **WHAT WOULD MAKE TODAY GREAT...**

INTENTION | **TODAY I WILL...**

GRATITUDE | **I'M GRATEFUL FOR...**

RELEASE | **I LET GO OF...**

SPACE | **ON MY MIND/IN MY HEART/ON MY SHOULDERS/ LIGHTING MY WAY...**

VISION | **WHAT WOULD MAKE TODAY GREAT...**

INTENTION | **TODAY I WILL...**

GRATITUDE | **I'M GRATEFUL FOR...**

RELEASE | **I LET GO OF...**

SPACE | **ON MY MIND/IN MY HEART/ON MY SHOULDERS/ LIGHTING MY WAY...**

VISION | **WHAT WOULD MAKE TODAY GREAT...**

INTENTION | **TODAY I WILL...**

GRATITUDE | **I'M GRATEFUL FOR...**

RELEASE | **I LET GO OF...**

SPACE | **ON MY MIND/IN MY HEART/ON MY SHOULDERS/
LIGHTING MY WAY...**

VISION | **WHAT WOULD MAKE TODAY GREAT...**

INTENTION | **TODAY I WILL...**

GRATITUDE | **I'M GRATEFUL FOR...**

RELEASE | **I LET GO OF...**

SPACE | **ON MY MIND/IN MY HEART/ON MY SHOULDERS/
LIGHTING MY WAY...**

VISION | **WHAT WOULD MAKE TODAY GREAT...**

INTENTION | **TODAY I WILL...**

GRATITUDE | **I'M GRATEFUL FOR...**

RELEASE | **I LET GO OF...**

SPACE | **ON MY MIND/IN MY HEART/ON MY SHOULDERS/ LIGHTING MY WAY...**

GRATEFUL FOR SAFETY

EMOTIONAL
WELLNESS

"Go inward and inquire, and you will see that all your miseries exist because you support them. Without your support nothing can exist. Because you give it energy, it exists; if you don't give it energy it cannot exist."

–OSHO,
EMOTIONAL WELLNESS:
TRANSFORMING FEAR,
ANGER, AND JEALOUSY
INTO CREATIVE ENERGY

REFLECTION

Emotional health is integral to our sense of safety because it keeps us centered even when things in our life are in upheaval. People who experience strong emotional health allow themselves to experience the full gamut of human emotions without getting stuck in any of them. The ability to see and be grateful for the good in oneself, others, and situations while acknowledging and accepting the negative helps you choose your responses to difficult situations.

SELF-INQUIRY INVITATIONS

* Look back over your last week. Quite likely, it was marked by highs and lows. Write about two or three things that you enjoyed despite your difficulties.
* What difficult emotions have you wrestled with recently? Were you nice to yourself as you experienced them? How can you show yourself lovingkindness during difficult times?
* Being optimistic doesn't mean always being happy. It means intentionally choosing your focus and response. Think of a current struggle in your life. Acknowledge it, and then write a new perspective by turning away from grumbles and replacing them with gratitude.

VISION | WHAT WOULD MAKE TODAY GREAT...

INTENTION | TODAY I WILL...

GRATITUDE | I'M GRATEFUL FOR...

RELEASE | I LET GO OF...

SPACE | ON MY MIND/IN MY HEART/ON MY SHOULDERS/
LIGHTING MY WAY...

VISION | **WHAT WOULD MAKE TODAY GREAT...**

INTENTION | **TODAY I WILL...**

GRATITUDE | **I'M GRATEFUL FOR...**

RELEASE | **I LET GO OF...**

SPACE | **ON MY MIND/IN MY HEART/ON MY SHOULDERS/
LIGHTING MY WAY...**

VISION | **WHAT WOULD MAKE TODAY GREAT...**

INTENTION | **TODAY I WILL...**

GRATITUDE | **I'M GRATEFUL FOR...**

RELEASE | **I LET GO OF...**

SPACE | **ON MY MIND/IN MY HEART/ON MY SHOULDERS/ LIGHTING MY WAY...**

VISION | **WHAT WOULD MAKE TODAY GREAT...**

INTENTION | **TODAY I WILL...**

GRATITUDE | **I'M GRATEFUL FOR...**

RELEASE | **I LET GO OF...**

SPACE | **ON MY MIND/IN MY HEART/ON MY SHOULDERS/ LIGHTING MY WAY...**

VISION | **WHAT WOULD MAKE TODAY GREAT...**

INTENTION | **TODAY I WILL...**

GRATITUDE | **I'M GRATEFUL FOR...**

RELEASE | **I LET GO OF...**

SPACE | **ON MY MIND/IN MY HEART/ON MY SHOULDERS/ LIGHTING MY WAY...**

VISION | **WHAT WOULD MAKE TODAY GREAT...**

INTENTION | **TODAY I WILL...**

GRATITUDE | **I'M GRATEFUL FOR...**

RELEASE | **I LET GO OF...**

SPACE | **ON MY MIND/IN MY HEART/ON MY SHOULDERS/ LIGHTING MY WAY...**

VISION | **WHAT WOULD MAKE TODAY GREAT...**

INTENTION | **TODAY I WILL...**

GRATITUDE | **I'M GRATEFUL FOR...**

RELEASE | **I LET GO OF...**

SPACE | **ON MY MIND/IN MY HEART/ON MY SHOULDERS/ LIGHTING MY WAY...**

VISION | **WHAT WOULD MAKE TODAY GREAT...**

INTENTION | **TODAY I WILL...**

GRATITUDE | **I'M GRATEFUL FOR...**

RELEASE | **I LET GO OF...**

SPACE | **ON MY MIND/IN MY HEART/ON MY SHOULDERS/
LIGHTING MY WAY...**

GRATEFUL FOR SAFETY

FINANCIAL HEALTH

"Wealth is the ability to fully experience life."

-HENRY DAVID THOREAU

REFLECTION

Financial health can mean different things. Everyone's personal definition of financial health varies, but it's a universal need to supply ourselves with the necessities—food, shelter, and clothing—to ensure our fundamental safety and survival. It's easy to take the essential element of financial health for granted. Make it a habit to pause and be grateful for what you are able to provide for yourself, focusing more on abundance than lack. On days when our financial future is uncertain or our prosperity is upended, consider the qualities you can cultivate within yourself to meet this challenge. Pragmatism, patience, perseverance, and openness have helped many people navigate financial hardships. Consider the qualities that speak to you.

SELF-INQUIRY INVITATIONS

* What does "wealth" mean to you? How much extra buying power, beyond paying for the basics, is enough for you to be content?
* If you had no financial restraints, what is one thing you would love to do? How can you use this to create a vision for a healthy financial future?
* A big component of financial health isn't how much money you have but how content you are with what you do have. Reflect on the things in your life right now—people, circumstances, or things—that are meaningful.

VISION | **WHAT WOULD MAKE TODAY GREAT...**

INTENTION | **TODAY I WILL...**

GRATITUDE | **I'M GRATEFUL FOR...**

RELEASE | **I LET GO OF...**

SPACE | **ON MY MIND/IN MY HEART/ON MY SHOULDERS/ LIGHTING MY WAY...**

VISION | **WHAT WOULD MAKE TODAY GREAT...**

INTENTION | **TODAY I WILL...**

GRATITUDE | **I'M GRATEFUL FOR...**

RELEASE | **I LET GO OF...**

SPACE | **ON MY MIND/IN MY HEART/ON MY SHOULDERS/ LIGHTING MY WAY...**

VISION | **WHAT WOULD MAKE TODAY GREAT...**

INTENTION | **TODAY I WILL...**

GRATITUDE | **I'M GRATEFUL FOR...**

RELEASE | **I LET GO OF...**

SPACE | **ON MY MIND/IN MY HEART/ON MY SHOULDERS/
LIGHTING MY WAY...**

VISION | **WHAT WOULD MAKE TODAY GREAT...**

INTENTION | **TODAY I WILL...**

GRATITUDE | **I'M GRATEFUL FOR...**

RELEASE | **I LET GO OF...**

SPACE | **ON MY MIND/IN MY HEART/ON MY SHOULDERS/ LIGHTING MY WAY...**

VISION | **WHAT WOULD MAKE TODAY GREAT...**

INTENTION | **TODAY I WILL...**

GRATITUDE | **I'M GRATEFUL FOR...**

RELEASE | **I LET GO OF...**

SPACE | **ON MY MIND/IN MY HEART/ON MY SHOULDERS/
LIGHTING MY WAY...**

VISION | **WHAT WOULD MAKE TODAY GREAT...**

INTENTION | **TODAY I WILL...**

GRATITUDE | **I'M GRATEFUL FOR...**

RELEASE | **I LET GO OF...**

SPACE | **ON MY MIND/IN MY HEART/ON MY SHOULDERS/
LIGHTING MY WAY...**

VISION | **WHAT WOULD MAKE TODAY GREAT...**

INTENTION | **TODAY I WILL...**

GRATITUDE | **I'M GRATEFUL FOR...**

RELEASE | **I LET GO OF...**

SPACE | **ON MY MIND/IN MY HEART/ON MY SHOULDERS/ LIGHTING MY WAY...**

VISION | **WHAT WOULD MAKE TODAY GREAT...**

INTENTION | **TODAY I WILL...**

GRATITUDE | **I'M GRATEFUL FOR...**

RELEASE | **I LET GO OF...**

SPACE | **ON MY MIND/IN MY HEART/ON MY SHOULDERS/
LIGHTING MY WAY...**

GRATEFUL FOR BELONGING

FAMILY

"*Look for the good, not the evil, in the conduct of members of the family.*"

—JEWISH PROVERB

REFLECTION

Family is a broad concept, not limited to our DNA or people dwelling under the same roof as us. A family is a strong bond of loved ones who support us through our lows and celebrate with us during our highs. Actively appreciating our family members for being warm fuzzies in a world that contains cold pricklies helps us open our hearts to receive and give love, seeing the strengths and forgiving the flaws in those we call family.

SELF-INQUIRY INVITATIONS

* What does *family* mean to you personally?
* What about your family do you value the most?
* Family members show love through more than just words. How do you know that you are cared for and supported?
* How do your family members know that you love them unconditionally? In what different ways do you express your love?

VISION | WHAT WOULD MAKE TODAY GREAT...

....

....

INTENTION | TODAY I WILL...

....

....

GRATITUDE | I'M GRATEFUL FOR...

....

....

RELEASE | I LET GO OF...

....

....

SPACE | ON MY MIND/IN MY HEART/ON MY SHOULDERS/
LIGHTING MY WAY...

....

....

....

....

VISION | WHAT WOULD MAKE TODAY GREAT...

INTENTION | TODAY I WILL...

GRATITUDE | I'M GRATEFUL FOR...

RELEASE | I LET GO OF...

SPACE | ON MY MIND/IN MY HEART/ON MY SHOULDERS/
LIGHTING MY WAY...

VISION | **WHAT WOULD MAKE TODAY GREAT...**

....

....

INTENTION | **TODAY I WILL...**

....

....

GRATITUDE | **I'M GRATEFUL FOR...**

....

....

RELEASE | **I LET GO OF...**

....

....

SPACE | **ON MY MIND/IN MY HEART/ON MY SHOULDERS/
LIGHTING MY WAY...**

....

....

....

....

....

VISION | **WHAT WOULD MAKE TODAY GREAT...**

INTENTION | **TODAY I WILL...**

GRATITUDE | **I'M GRATEFUL FOR...**

RELEASE | **I LET GO OF...**

SPACE | **ON MY MIND/IN MY HEART/ON MY SHOULDERS/
LIGHTING MY WAY...**

VISION | WHAT WOULD MAKE TODAY GREAT...

INTENTION | TODAY I WILL...

GRATITUDE | I'M GRATEFUL FOR...

RELEASE | I LET GO OF...

SPACE | ON MY MIND/IN MY HEART/ON MY SHOULDERS/
LIGHTING MY WAY...

VISION | WHAT WOULD MAKE TODAY GREAT...

INTENTION | TODAY I WILL...

GRATITUDE | I'M GRATEFUL FOR...

RELEASE | I LET GO OF...

SPACE | ON MY MIND/IN MY HEART/ON MY SHOULDERS/
LIGHTING MY WAY...

VISION | WHAT WOULD MAKE TODAY GREAT...

INTENTION | TODAY I WILL...

GRATITUDE | I'M GRATEFUL FOR...

RELEASE | I LET GO OF...

SPACE | ON MY MIND/IN MY HEART/ON MY SHOULDERS/
LIGHTING MY WAY...

VISION | **WHAT WOULD MAKE TODAY GREAT...**

INTENTION | **TODAY I WILL...**

GRATITUDE | **I'M GRATEFUL FOR...**

RELEASE | **I LET GO OF...**

SPACE | **ON MY MIND/IN MY HEART/ON MY SHOULDERS/
LIGHTING MY WAY...**

GRATEFUL FOR BELONGING

COMMUNITY

*"Sticks in a bundle
are unbreakable."*

–KENYAN PROVERB

REFLECTION

Whether we are outgoing and gregarious or introverted and reflective, we're still social beings who need connection to those around us. Belonging to a community, big or small, brings many benefits: a sense of being accepted and valued for who we are, and validation for our unique strengths and contributions. Being part of a community can be a source of joy, growth, comfort, and inspiration.

SELF-INQUIRY INVITATIONS

* What interests you in your community? What would it be like to connect with a like-minded group?
* What strengths do you have to offer your neighborhood or wider community?
* What can you do to foster a deeper connection with your friends, coworkers, or other members of your community?

VISION | WHAT WOULD MAKE TODAY GREAT...

INTENTION | TODAY I WILL...

GRATITUDE | I'M GRATEFUL FOR...

RELEASE | I LET GO OF...

SPACE | ON MY MIND/IN MY HEART/ON MY SHOULDERS/
LIGHTING MY WAY...

VISION | WHAT WOULD MAKE TODAY GREAT...

INTENTION | TODAY I WILL...

GRATITUDE | I'M GRATEFUL FOR...

RELEASE | I LET GO OF...

SPACE | ON MY MIND/IN MY HEART/ON MY SHOULDERS/
LIGHTING MY WAY...

VISION | WHAT WOULD MAKE TODAY GREAT...

INTENTION | TODAY I WILL...

GRATITUDE | I'M GRATEFUL FOR...

RELEASE | I LET GO OF...

SPACE | ON MY MIND/IN MY HEART/ON MY SHOULDERS/
LIGHTING MY WAY...

VISION | **WHAT WOULD MAKE TODAY GREAT...**

INTENTION | **TODAY I WILL...**

GRATITUDE | **I'M GRATEFUL FOR...**

RELEASE | **I LET GO OF...**

SPACE | **ON MY MIND/IN MY HEART/ON MY SHOULDERS/
LIGHTING MY WAY...**

VISION | WHAT WOULD MAKE TODAY GREAT...

INTENTION | TODAY I WILL...

GRATITUDE | I'M GRATEFUL FOR...

RELEASE | I LET GO OF...

SPACE | ON MY MIND/IN MY HEART/ON MY SHOULDERS/
LIGHTING MY WAY...

VISION | WHAT WOULD MAKE TODAY GREAT...

INTENTION | TODAY I WILL...

GRATITUDE | I'M GRATEFUL FOR...

RELEASE | I LET GO OF...

SPACE | ON MY MIND/IN MY HEART/ON MY SHOULDERS/
LIGHTING MY WAY...

VISION | WHAT WOULD MAKE TODAY GREAT...

....

....

INTENTION | TODAY I WILL...

....

....

GRATITUDE | I'M GRATEFUL FOR...

....

....

RELEASE | I LET GO OF...

....

....

SPACE | ON MY MIND/IN MY HEART/ON MY SHOULDERS/
LIGHTING MY WAY...

....

....

....

....

....

VISION | **WHAT WOULD MAKE TODAY GREAT...**

INTENTION | **TODAY I WILL...**

GRATITUDE | **I'M GRATEFUL FOR...**

RELEASE | **I LET GO OF...**

SPACE | **ON MY MIND/IN MY HEART/ON MY SHOULDERS/ LIGHTING MY WAY...**

FRIENDSHIP AND INTIMACY

"I love my friends
neither with my heart
nor with my mind, just
in case my heart might
stop and mind can forget.
I love them with my soul.
Soul never stops or forgets."

-RUMI

REFLECTION

Whether we're introverts or extroverts, are content with more time in solitude or thrive in groups, we all need friendship and intimacy. These relationships nurture us on a deep level. When we connect closely with another person, we experience acceptance for who we are and inspiration to grow into someone better. In friendships, we gift each other with warmth, caring, compassion, and mutual understanding. Friends elevate each other, laugh together, and cry together. Together, we don't face life alone.

SELF-INQUIRY INVITATIONS

* Reflect on a friendship you have, whether it's someone you spend a lot of time with or someone who lives far away that you connect with only occasionally. What makes this relationship special to you?
* How do you let your loved ones know that you care?
* How do you know that you are loved?
* What is one spontaneous, small act of kindness you can do today for a friend to brighten their day?

VISION | WHAT WOULD MAKE TODAY GREAT...

INTENTION | TODAY I WILL...

GRATITUDE | I'M GRATEFUL FOR...

RELEASE | I LET GO OF...

SPACE | ON MY MIND/IN MY HEART/ON MY SHOULDERS/
LIGHTING MY WAY...

VISION | WHAT WOULD MAKE TODAY GREAT...

INTENTION | TODAY I WILL...

GRATITUDE | I'M GRATEFUL FOR...

RELEASE | I LET GO OF...

SPACE | ON MY MIND/IN MY HEART/ON MY SHOULDERS/
LIGHTING MY WAY...

VISION | **WHAT WOULD MAKE TODAY GREAT...**

INTENTION | **TODAY I WILL...**

GRATITUDE | **I'M GRATEFUL FOR...**

RELEASE | **I LET GO OF...**

SPACE | **ON MY MIND/IN MY HEART/ON MY SHOULDERS/ LIGHTING MY WAY...**

VISION | **WHAT WOULD MAKE TODAY GREAT...**

INTENTION | **TODAY I WILL...**

GRATITUDE | **I'M GRATEFUL FOR...**

RELEASE | **I LET GO OF...**

SPACE | **ON MY MIND/IN MY HEART/ON MY SHOULDERS/ LIGHTING MY WAY...**

VISION | WHAT WOULD MAKE TODAY GREAT...

INTENTION | TODAY I WILL...

GRATITUDE | I'M GRATEFUL FOR...

RELEASE | I LET GO OF...

SPACE | ON MY MIND/IN MY HEART/ON MY SHOULDERS/
LIGHTING MY WAY...

VISION | WHAT WOULD MAKE TODAY GREAT...

INTENTION | TODAY I WILL...

GRATITUDE | I'M GRATEFUL FOR...

RELEASE | I LET GO OF...

SPACE | ON MY MIND/IN MY HEART/ON MY SHOULDERS/
LIGHTING MY WAY...

VISION | WHAT WOULD MAKE TODAY GREAT...

....

....

INTENTION | TODAY I WILL...

....

....

GRATITUDE | I'M GRATEFUL FOR...

....

....

RELEASE | I LET GO OF...

....

....

SPACE | ON MY MIND/IN MY HEART/ON MY SHOULDERS/
LIGHTING MY WAY...

....

....

....

....

....

VISION | **WHAT WOULD MAKE TODAY GREAT...**

....

....

INTENTION | **TODAY I WILL...**

....

....

GRATITUDE | **I'M GRATEFUL FOR...**

....

....

RELEASE | **I LET GO OF...**

....

....

SPACE | **ON MY MIND/IN MY HEART/ON MY SHOULDERS/
LIGHTING MY WAY...**

....

....

....

....

....

GRATEFUL FOR GROWTH

SELF-CONFIDENCE

"Trust yourself. Create the kind of self that you will be happy to live with all your life. Make the most of yourself by fanning the tiny, inner sparks of possibility into flames of achievement."

–GOLDA MEIR

REFLECTION

Far from ego, self-confidence is an acknowledgment of all of your strengths and weaknesses. Knowing who you are, fully and completely, leads to a healthy self-concept that is necessary for self-acceptance and self-compassion. Then, you can let go of the fear of being judged and live with an open mind and heart, a sense of curiosity, and the courage to try new things and take risks for success. Self-confidence is the freedom to grow and blossom.

SELF-INQUIRY INVITATIONS

* Imagine you are starting your dream job, and your good friend already works at the same place. She is introducing you to coworkers. What will she say about you?
* Complete this sentence positively. "I am someone who_____." ("I am someone who is honest with people, and I'm proud that people can believe what I say.")
* What do you gain by being hard on yourself, for berating yourself for your imperfections? How will your day be different when you accept that we all have room to learn and grow—and then focus on your strengths?

VISION | **WHAT WOULD MAKE TODAY GREAT...**

INTENTION | **TODAY I WILL...**

GRATITUDE | **I'M GRATEFUL FOR...**

RELEASE | **I LET GO OF...**

SPACE | **ON MY MIND/IN MY HEART/ON MY SHOULDERS/ LIGHTING MY WAY...**

VISION | **WHAT WOULD MAKE TODAY GREAT...**

INTENTION | **TODAY I WILL...**

GRATITUDE | **I'M GRATEFUL FOR...**

RELEASE | **I LET GO OF...**

SPACE | **ON MY MIND/IN MY HEART/ON MY SHOULDERS/ LIGHTING MY WAY...**

VISION | **WHAT WOULD MAKE TODAY GREAT...**

INTENTION | **TODAY I WILL...**

GRATITUDE | **I'M GRATEFUL FOR...**

RELEASE | **I LET GO OF...**

SPACE | **ON MY MIND/IN MY HEART/ON MY SHOULDERS/ LIGHTING MY WAY...**

VISION | **WHAT WOULD MAKE TODAY GREAT...**

INTENTION | **TODAY I WILL...**

GRATITUDE | **I'M GRATEFUL FOR...**

RELEASE | **I LET GO OF...**

SPACE | **ON MY MIND/IN MY HEART/ON MY SHOULDERS/ LIGHTING MY WAY...**

VISION | **WHAT WOULD MAKE TODAY GREAT...**

INTENTION | **TODAY I WILL...**

GRATITUDE | **I'M GRATEFUL FOR...**

RELEASE | **I LET GO OF...**

SPACE | **ON MY MIND/IN MY HEART/ON MY SHOULDERS/
LIGHTING MY WAY...**

VISION | **WHAT WOULD MAKE TODAY GREAT...**

INTENTION | **TODAY I WILL...**

GRATITUDE | **I'M GRATEFUL FOR...**

RELEASE | **I LET GO OF...**

SPACE | **ON MY MIND/IN MY HEART/ON MY SHOULDERS/
LIGHTING MY WAY...**

VISION | **WHAT WOULD MAKE TODAY GREAT...**

INTENTION | **TODAY I WILL...**

GRATITUDE | **I'M GRATEFUL FOR...**

RELEASE | **I LET GO OF...**

SPACE | **ON MY MIND/IN MY HEART/ON MY SHOULDERS/ LIGHTING MY WAY...**

VISION | **WHAT WOULD MAKE TODAY GREAT...**

INTENTION | **TODAY I WILL...**

GRATITUDE | **I'M GRATEFUL FOR...**

RELEASE | **I LET GO OF...**

SPACE | **ON MY MIND/IN MY HEART/ON MY SHOULDERS/ LIGHTING MY WAY...**

GRATEFUL FOR GROWTH

SKILLS, EDUCATION, AND CAREER

"*We work to become,
not to acquire.*"

—ELBERT HUBBARD

REFLECTION

We all spend a significant amount of time in school or at work. Even if your work is at home, you still spend a huge portion of your life dedicated to it. Therefore, it's vital to our well-being that we like what we do. Work and studies aren't just about getting a paycheck now or in the future. They're about becoming who we want to be and using our strengths to create meaning, fulfillment, and purpose.

SELF-INQUIRY INVITATIONS

* How do you use your skills in what you do every day?
* What little changes can you make at school or work to increase your satisfaction?
* Reflect here on why you are grateful for the skills you have acquired, the training and education you have received, and the path you have taken so far in life.

VISION | **WHAT WOULD MAKE TODAY GREAT...**

INTENTION | **TODAY I WILL...**

GRATITUDE | **I'M GRATEFUL FOR...**

RELEASE | **I LET GO OF...**

SPACE | **ON MY MIND/IN MY HEART/ON MY SHOULDERS/
LIGHTING MY WAY...**

VISION | **WHAT WOULD MAKE TODAY GREAT...**

INTENTION | **TODAY I WILL...**

GRATITUDE | **I'M GRATEFUL FOR...**

RELEASE | **I LET GO OF...**

SPACE | **ON MY MIND/IN MY HEART/ON MY SHOULDERS/
LIGHTING MY WAY...**

VISION | **WHAT WOULD MAKE TODAY GREAT...**

INTENTION | **TODAY I WILL...**

GRATITUDE | **I'M GRATEFUL FOR...**

RELEASE | **I LET GO OF...**

SPACE | **ON MY MIND/IN MY HEART/ON MY SHOULDERS/
LIGHTING MY WAY...**

VISION | **WHAT WOULD MAKE TODAY GREAT...**

INTENTION | **TODAY I WILL...**

GRATITUDE | **I'M GRATEFUL FOR...**

RELEASE | **I LET GO OF...**

SPACE | **ON MY MIND/IN MY HEART/ON MY SHOULDERS/ LIGHTING MY WAY...**

VISION | WHAT WOULD MAKE TODAY GREAT...

INTENTION | TODAY I WILL...

GRATITUDE | I'M GRATEFUL FOR...

RELEASE | I LET GO OF...

SPACE | ON MY MIND/IN MY HEART/ON MY SHOULDERS/
LIGHTING MY WAY...

VISION | WHAT WOULD MAKE TODAY GREAT...

INTENTION | TODAY I WILL...

GRATITUDE | I'M GRATEFUL FOR...

RELEASE | I LET GO OF...

SPACE | ON MY MIND/IN MY HEART/ON MY SHOULDERS/
LIGHTING MY WAY...

VISION | **WHAT WOULD MAKE TODAY GREAT...**

INTENTION | **TODAY I WILL...**

GRATITUDE | **I'M GRATEFUL FOR...**

RELEASE | **I LET GO OF...**

SPACE | **ON MY MIND/IN MY HEART/ON MY SHOULDERS/
LIGHTING MY WAY...**

VISION | **WHAT WOULD MAKE TODAY GREAT...**

INTENTION | **TODAY I WILL...**

GRATITUDE | **I'M GRATEFUL FOR...**

RELEASE | **I LET GO OF...**

SPACE | **ON MY MIND/IN MY HEART/ON MY SHOULDERS/
LIGHTING MY WAY...**

GRATEFUL FOR GROWTH

CHALLENGES AND TRIUMPHS

*"In the depth of winter,
I finally learned that
within me there lay an
invincible summer."*

—ALBERT CAMUS

REFLECTION

When a butterfly is ready to emerge from its chrysalis, it must struggle to free itself. It puts forth a tremendous effort, punching through the wall with its legs, twisting and wriggling loose, and working to move and unfurl its smooshed, crinkled wings. This struggle strengthens the butterfly so it can soar. If you were to help a butterfly by peeling away the chrysalis and gently extracting it, the butterfly wouldn't grow strong—it would wither and die. Like a butterfly, you face challenges so you can soar.

SELF-INQUIRY INVITATIONS

* Reflect on a current challenge. What greater purpose might it be serving?
* We can think of challenges as calls to action. What steps can you take today to manage an obstacle you're facing?
* Describe how you have felt when you triumphed over a hardship. List words you could use to convey the positive feelings and thoughts you had about yourself.
* What is available to you to help you triumph in your life right now? Think of people, resources, and your own inner reserves and sources of strength.

VISION | WHAT WOULD MAKE TODAY GREAT...

INTENTION | TODAY I WILL...

GRATITUDE | I'M GRATEFUL FOR...

RELEASE | I LET GO OF...

SPACE | ON MY MIND/IN MY HEART/ON MY SHOULDERS/
LIGHTING MY WAY...

VISION | WHAT WOULD MAKE TODAY GREAT...

INTENTION | TODAY I WILL...

GRATITUDE | I'M GRATEFUL FOR...

RELEASE | I LET GO OF...

SPACE | ON MY MIND/IN MY HEART/ON MY SHOULDERS/
LIGHTING MY WAY...

VISION | **WHAT WOULD MAKE TODAY GREAT...**

INTENTION | **TODAY I WILL...**

GRATITUDE | **I'M GRATEFUL FOR...**

RELEASE | **I LET GO OF...**

SPACE | **ON MY MIND/IN MY HEART/ON MY SHOULDERS/
LIGHTING MY WAY...**

VISION | **WHAT WOULD MAKE TODAY GREAT...**

INTENTION | **TODAY I WILL...**

GRATITUDE | **I'M GRATEFUL FOR...**

RELEASE | **I LET GO OF...**

SPACE | **ON MY MIND/IN MY HEART/ON MY SHOULDERS/
LIGHTING MY WAY...**

VISION | **WHAT WOULD MAKE TODAY GREAT...**

INTENTION | **TODAY I WILL...**

GRATITUDE | **I'M GRATEFUL FOR...**

RELEASE | **I LET GO OF...**

SPACE | **ON MY MIND/IN MY HEART/ON MY SHOULDERS/ LIGHTING MY WAY...**

VISION | WHAT WOULD MAKE TODAY GREAT...

INTENTION | TODAY I WILL...

GRATITUDE | I'M GRATEFUL FOR...

RELEASE | I LET GO OF...

SPACE | ON MY MIND/IN MY HEART/ON MY SHOULDERS/
LIGHTING MY WAY...

VISION | **WHAT WOULD MAKE TODAY GREAT...**

INTENTION | **TODAY I WILL...**

GRATITUDE | **I'M GRATEFUL FOR...**

RELEASE | **I LET GO OF...**

SPACE | **ON MY MIND/IN MY HEART/ON MY SHOULDERS/ LIGHTING MY WAY...**

VISION | WHAT WOULD MAKE TODAY GREAT...

INTENTION | TODAY I WILL...

GRATITUDE | I'M GRATEFUL FOR...

RELEASE | I LET GO OF...

SPACE | ON MY MIND/IN MY HEART/ON MY SHOULDERS/
LIGHTING MY WAY...

GRATEFUL FOR VISION

DREAMS

"*Everything can be taken from a man but one thing: the last of the human freedoms—to choose one's attitude in any given set of circumstances, to choose one's own way.*"

—VIKTOR E. FRANKL,
MAN'S SEARCH FOR MEANING

REFLECTION

Our hopes and dreams for ourselves are the seeds we nurture in order to grow into the people we want to be. Your dreams are your conceptualization of what makes your life worth living. They're about hope for the future and the belief in yourself that you have the power to shape your life. Dreams are also rooted in the present and the actions you take every day to realize them.

SELF-INQUIRY INVITATIONS

* Describe one of your biggest dreams for your life.
* What kind of person are you in your dreams? Call to mind someone for whom you have a deep respect, and describe their qualities you'd like to emulate.
* Think of a chore at work or home that is bogging you down right now. How can you change the way you think about it so that it becomes part of your greater life plan?

VISION | WHAT WOULD MAKE TODAY GREAT...

....

....

INTENTION | TODAY I WILL...

....

....

GRATITUDE | I'M GRATEFUL FOR...

....

....

RELEASE | I LET GO OF...

....

....

SPACE | ON MY MIND/IN MY HEART/ON MY SHOULDERS/
LIGHTING MY WAY...

....

....

....

....

....

VISION | WHAT WOULD MAKE TODAY GREAT...

INTENTION | TODAY I WILL...

GRATITUDE | I'M GRATEFUL FOR...

RELEASE | I LET GO OF...

SPACE | ON MY MIND/IN MY HEART/ON MY SHOULDERS/
LIGHTING MY WAY...

VISION | **WHAT WOULD MAKE TODAY GREAT...**

INTENTION | **TODAY I WILL...**

GRATITUDE | **I'M GRATEFUL FOR...**

RELEASE | **I LET GO OF...**

SPACE | **ON MY MIND/IN MY HEART/ON MY SHOULDERS/
LIGHTING MY WAY...**

VISION | **WHAT WOULD MAKE TODAY GREAT...**

INTENTION | **TODAY I WILL...**

GRATITUDE | **I'M GRATEFUL FOR...**

RELEASE | **I LET GO OF...**

SPACE | **ON MY MIND/IN MY HEART/ON MY SHOULDERS/
LIGHTING MY WAY...**

VISION | WHAT WOULD MAKE TODAY GREAT...

INTENTION | TODAY I WILL...

GRATITUDE | I'M GRATEFUL FOR...

RELEASE | I LET GO OF...

SPACE | ON MY MIND/IN MY HEART/ON MY SHOULDERS/
LIGHTING MY WAY...

VISION | WHAT WOULD MAKE TODAY GREAT...

INTENTION | TODAY I WILL...

GRATITUDE | I'M GRATEFUL FOR...

RELEASE | I LET GO OF...

SPACE | ON MY MIND/IN MY HEART/ON MY SHOULDERS/
LIGHTING MY WAY...

VISION | **WHAT WOULD MAKE TODAY GREAT...**

....

....

INTENTION | **TODAY I WILL...**

....

....

GRATITUDE | **I'M GRATEFUL FOR...**

....

....

RELEASE | **I LET GO OF...**

....

....

SPACE | **ON MY MIND/IN MY HEART/ON MY SHOULDERS/ LIGHTING MY WAY...**

....

....

....

....

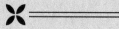

VISION | **WHAT WOULD MAKE TODAY GREAT...**

INTENTION | **TODAY I WILL...**

GRATITUDE | **I'M GRATEFUL FOR...**

RELEASE | **I LET GO OF...**

SPACE | **ON MY MIND/IN MY HEART/ON MY SHOULDERS/ LIGHTING MY WAY...**

GRATEFUL FOR VISION

CALLING
AND PURPOSE

"I'm always thinking about creating. My future starts when I wake up every morning . . . Every day I find something creative to do with my life."

–MILES DAVIS,
MILES: THE AUTOBIOGRAPHY

REFLECTION

Did you leap from your bed this morning, ready to seize a fresh parcel of time and possibility? If not, today's theme will help you contemplate what inspires you and gives you purpose. We all have a to-do list. But waiting for us on the other side of grocery shopping and cleaning the dishes and making phone calls, patiently or impatiently, is our own soul. Today's questions are about finding your deeper meaning every day.

SELF-INQUIRY INVITATIONS

✱ What would make today meaningful for you?
✱ What part of you is waiting to be seen and expressed?
✱ What small actions can you take today to feel alive and vibrant?
✱ What does purpose feel like to you?

VISION | WHAT WOULD MAKE TODAY GREAT...

....

....

INTENTION | TODAY I WILL...

....

....

GRATITUDE | I'M GRATEFUL FOR...

....

....

RELEASE | I LET GO OF...

....

....

SPACE | ON MY MIND/IN MY HEART/ON MY SHOULDERS/
LIGHTING MY WAY...

....

....

....

....

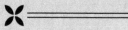

VISION | WHAT WOULD MAKE TODAY GREAT...

INTENTION | TODAY I WILL...

GRATITUDE | I'M GRATEFUL FOR...

RELEASE | I LET GO OF...

SPACE | ON MY MIND/IN MY HEART/ON MY SHOULDERS/
LIGHTING MY WAY...

VISION | **WHAT WOULD MAKE TODAY GREAT...**

INTENTION | **TODAY I WILL...**

GRATITUDE | **I'M GRATEFUL FOR...**

RELEASE | **I LET GO OF...**

SPACE | **ON MY MIND/IN MY HEART/ON MY SHOULDERS/
LIGHTING MY WAY...**

VISION | **WHAT WOULD MAKE TODAY GREAT...**

INTENTION | **TODAY I WILL...**

GRATITUDE | **I'M GRATEFUL FOR...**

RELEASE | **I LET GO OF...**

SPACE | **ON MY MIND/IN MY HEART/ON MY SHOULDERS/
LIGHTING MY WAY...**

VISION | WHAT WOULD MAKE TODAY GREAT...

INTENTION | TODAY I WILL...

GRATITUDE | I'M GRATEFUL FOR...

RELEASE | I LET GO OF...

SPACE | ON MY MIND/IN MY HEART/ON MY SHOULDERS/
LIGHTING MY WAY...

VISION | **WHAT WOULD MAKE TODAY GREAT...**

INTENTION | **TODAY I WILL...**

GRATITUDE | **I'M GRATEFUL FOR...**

RELEASE | **I LET GO OF...**

SPACE | **ON MY MIND/IN MY HEART/ON MY SHOULDERS/ LIGHTING MY WAY...**

VISION | WHAT WOULD MAKE TODAY GREAT...

INTENTION | TODAY I WILL...

GRATITUDE | I'M GRATEFUL FOR...

RELEASE | I LET GO OF...

SPACE | ON MY MIND/IN MY HEART/ON MY SHOULDERS/ LIGHTING MY WAY...

VISION | **WHAT WOULD MAKE TODAY GREAT...**

INTENTION | **TODAY I WILL...**

GRATITUDE | **I'M GRATEFUL FOR...**

RELEASE | **I LET GO OF...**

SPACE | **ON MY MIND/IN MY HEART/ON MY SHOULDERS/ LIGHTING MY WAY...**

GRATEFUL FOR VISION

SERVICE TO
THE WORLD

"*Only the development of compassion and understanding for others can bring us the tranquility and happiness we all seek.*"

−HIS HOLINESS THE 14TH DALAI LAMA

REFLECTION

Research in positive psychology reveals that when we use our unique strengths in service to others and to things bigger than ourselves, we cultivate a deep sense of meaning and create a life worth living. Acts of altruism, big and small, that improve others' lives also improve our own. When you do things for others, you pull yourself out of your own head and into your real life, a quality that you create moment by moment.

SELF-INQUIRY INVITATIONS

* Reflect on your gifts, strengths, and talents. How can you use one of them today to enhance someone else's day?
* Challenge yourself. How many small random acts of kindness do you think you can do today?
* Who can you spend time with mindfully today?
* Volunteering is a great way to connect with and help others. How or where might you give your time and energy in a way that aligns with your sense of purpose?

VISION | **WHAT WOULD MAKE TODAY GREAT...**

....

....

INTENTION | **TODAY I WILL...**

....

....

GRATITUDE | **I'M GRATEFUL FOR...**

....

....

RELEASE | **I LET GO OF...**

....

....

SPACE | **ON MY MIND/IN MY HEART/ON MY SHOULDERS/
LIGHTING MY WAY...**

....

....

....

....

....

VISION | WHAT WOULD MAKE TODAY GREAT...

INTENTION | TODAY I WILL...

GRATITUDE | I'M GRATEFUL FOR...

RELEASE | I LET GO OF...

SPACE | ON MY MIND/IN MY HEART/ON MY SHOULDERS/
LIGHTING MY WAY...

VISION | **WHAT WOULD MAKE TODAY GREAT...**

....

....

INTENTION | **TODAY I WILL...**

....

....

GRATITUDE | **I'M GRATEFUL FOR...**

....

....

RELEASE | **I LET GO OF...**

....

....

SPACE | **ON MY MIND/IN MY HEART/ON MY SHOULDERS/
LIGHTING MY WAY...**

....

....

....

....

....

VISION | **WHAT WOULD MAKE TODAY GREAT...**

INTENTION | **TODAY I WILL...**

GRATITUDE | **I'M GRATEFUL FOR...**

RELEASE | **I LET GO OF...**

SPACE | **ON MY MIND/IN MY HEART/ON MY SHOULDERS/
LIGHTING MY WAY...**

VISION | WHAT WOULD MAKE TODAY GREAT...

....

....

INTENTION | TODAY I WILL...

....

....

GRATITUDE | I'M GRATEFUL FOR...

....

....

RELEASE | I LET GO OF...

....

....

SPACE | ON MY MIND/IN MY HEART/ON MY SHOULDERS/
LIGHTING MY WAY...

....

....

....

....

....

VISION | WHAT WOULD MAKE TODAY GREAT...

INTENTION | TODAY I WILL...

GRATITUDE | I'M GRATEFUL FOR...

RELEASE | I LET GO OF...

SPACE | ON MY MIND/IN MY HEART/ON MY SHOULDERS/
LIGHTING MY WAY...

VISION | **WHAT WOULD MAKE TODAY GREAT...**

INTENTION | **TODAY I WILL...**

GRATITUDE | **I'M GRATEFUL FOR...**

RELEASE | **I LET GO OF...**

SPACE | **ON MY MIND/IN MY HEART/ON MY SHOULDERS/ LIGHTING MY WAY...**

VISION | **WHAT WOULD MAKE TODAY GREAT...**

INTENTION | **TODAY I WILL...**

GRATITUDE | **I'M GRATEFUL FOR...**

RELEASE | **I LET GO OF...**

SPACE | **ON MY MIND/IN MY HEART/ON MY SHOULDERS/
LIGHTING MY WAY...**

RESOURCES

Cultivating an attitude of gratitude and a regular journaling habit can be a joyful, lifelong process. Regular expression of gratitude and intentional journaling will develop and shape your perspective. The practice allows you to identify and cultivate a sense of meaning and purpose that leads to new perspectives and actions for a life of deep well-being. These resources are available to support you on your path.

ARTICLES ABOUT GRATITUDE

Carpenter, Derrick. "The Science Behind Gratitude (and How It Can Change Your Life)." happify.com/hd/the-science-behind-gratitude

Glass, Kelly. "This 5-Minute Gratitude Exercise Can Help Ease Stress (and Support Your Immune System)." livestrong.com/article/13 726036-gratitude-exercise-reduce-stress

Goldstein, Elisha. "Rewire Your Brain for Joy with a Simple Gratitude Practice." mindful.org/power-boost-your-gratitude-practice

Greater Good Magazine. "Gratitude Defined." greatergood.berkeley. edu/topic/gratitude/definition

Miller, Kori D. "14 Health Benefits of Practicing Gratitude According to Science." positivepsychology.com/benefits-of-gratitude

Mindful.org. "How to Practice Gratitude." mindful.org/an-introductio n-to-mindful-gratitude

ARTICLES ABOUT JOURNALING

Ackerman, MSc, Courtney E. "Gratitude Journal: A Collection of 67 Templates, Ideas, and Apps for Your Diary." positivepsychology.com/ gratitude-journal

Purcell, LCSW, CEAP, Maud. "The Health Benefits of Journaling." psychcentral.com/lib/the-health-benefits-of-journaling

Scott, MS, Elizabeth. "The Benefits of Journaling for Stress Management." verywellmind.com/the-benefits-of-journaling-for-stress-management-3144611

Marsh, Jason. "Tips for Keeping a Gratitude Journal." greatergood.berkeley.edu/article/item/tips_for_keeping_a_gratitude_journal

Smith, Emma-Marie. "Why Keep a Positivity Journal?" healthyplace.com/self-help/positivity/why-keep-a-positivity-journal

ONLINE JOURNALING AND/ OR GRATITUDE EXPERIENCES

JOURNALING.COM. This is an online journaling community that provides a wealth of information and resources for journaling practice. They offer five paths, or focus areas, and users can choose one or more to fit their needs: emotional well-being, creativity, productivity, physical health, and mindfulness.

FACEBOOK. You can find numerous groups dedicated to gratitude or journaling on this popular social media platform. Type "gratitude groups" or "journaling groups" into the search box and choose a group that suit your personality and preferences.

MEETUP. This online platform connects like-minded people in communities across the globe. You can use MeetUp.com to search for gratitude and journaling groups in or near your community. Such groups offer the power of encouragement and shared experience.

APPS

365 GRATITUDE. This app is a gratitude journal and more. Users receive daily inspirations and coaching and can complete a daily gratitude journal or gratitude jar, track their moods, play games, and participate

in a self-care community. It's free to download for iOS and Android with in-app purchases. 365gratitudejournal.com

DAY ONE. This daily journaling app helps you record important thoughts, feelings, and events by journaling and uploading photos. Easily record, organize, and share your thoughts and gratitudes. Available for iOS and Android. dayoneapp.com

GRATITUDE. This free app for iOS and Android is a simple gratitude journal that offers inspiration and a place to record grateful thoughts or photos. You can even send a note of thanks to people through this app. gratefulness.me

MY OTHER JOURNALS TO OVERCOME ANXIETY AND ENHANCE WELL-BEING

The 5-Minute Anxiety Relief Journal

The Mindfulness Journal for Anxiety

REFERENCES

Alliance for Transforming the Lives of Children. "Benefits of Community." Connected Couples-Thriving Families. Accessed April 4, 2020. ConnectedandThriving.org/hope/benefits-of-community.

Cheng, Sheung-Tak, Pui Ki Tsui, and John H. M. Lam. "Improving Mental Health in Health Care Practitioners: Randomized Controlled Trial of a Gratitude Intervention." *Journal of Consulting and Clinical Psychology* 83, no. 1 (2015): 177-86. doi:10.1037/a0037895.

Cherra, Kendra. "The 5 Levels of Maslow's Hierarchy of Needs." verywell mind. Updated December 3, 2019. verywellmind.com/what-is-maslows-hierarchy-of-needs-4136760.

Emmons, Robert A., and Michael E. McCullough. "Counting Blessings versus Burdens: An Experimental Investigation of Gratitude and Subjective Well-Being in Daily Life." *Journal of Personality and* Social *Psychology* 84, no. 2 (2003): 377-89. doi:10.1037/0022-3514.84.2.377.

Exploring Your Mind. "The 5 Love Languages, According to Gary Chapman." February 28, 2018. ExploringYourMind.com/5-love-languages-gary-chapman.

Guerra, Julia. "16 Benefits of Gratitude, According to Science & Mental Health Experts." mbgmindfulness. Updated September 10, 2019. mindbodygreen.com/0-6823/10-Benefits-of-Gratitude.html.

Harvard Medical School Special Health Report: Positive Psychology. "Finding Your Life's Meaning." Boston: Harvard Medical School, 2019.

Harvard Medical School Special Health Report: Positive Psychology. "Flow: Getting Engaged and Absorbed." Boston: Harvard Medical School, 2019.

Jaworski, Margaret. "The Negativity Bias: Why the Bad Stuff Sticks." Psycom. Updated February 19, 2020. Psycom.net/negativity-bias.

Miller, Kori D. "14 Health Benefits of Practicing Gratitude According to Science." PositivePsychology.com. Updated April 2, 2020. Positive psychology.com/benefits-of-gratitude.

MindWise Innovations. "The Importance of Social Connections." Accessed April 4, 2020. MindWise.org/blog/uncategorized /the-importance-of-social-connection.

Moore, Catherine. "What Is the Negativity Bias and How Can It Be Overcome?" PositivePsychology.com. December 30, 2019. Positive Psychology.com/3-steps-negativity-bias.

National Institutes of Health (NIH). "Practicing Gratitude: Ways to Improve Positivity." NIH News in Health. March 2019. NewsinHealth .nih.gov/2019/03/practicing-gratitude.

Peterson, Tanya J. "What Is Emotional Wellness?" HealthyPlace .com. Updated July 25, 2019. HealthyPlace.com/self-help /self-help-information/what-emotional-wellness.

Peterson, Tanya J. "What Does It Mean to Be Emotionally Healthy?" HealthyPlace.com. Updated October 23, 2019. HealthyPlace .com/self-help/self-help-information/what-does-it-mean -be-emotionally-healthy.

Reiman Gardens. "How Do Butterflies/Moths Spread Their Wings After Emerging?" Iowa State University. Accessed May 1, 2020. Reiman Gardens.com/butterfly/butterfliesmoths-spread-wings-emerging.

U.C. Davis. "Emotional Wellness." Accessed April 25, 2020. SHCS.uc davis.edu/wellness/emotional.

VIA Institute on Character. "The 24 Character Strengths." Accessed April 5, 2020. VIACharacter.org/character-strengths.

Wong, Y. Joel, Jesse Owen, Nicole T. Gabana, Joshua W. Brown, Sydney McInnis, Paul Toth, and Lynn Gilman. "Does gratitude writing improve the mental health of psychotherapy clients? Evidence from a randomized controlled trial." *Psychotherapy Research* 28, no. 2 (2018): 192-202.doi:10.1080/10503307.2016.1169332.

ABOUT THE AUTHOR

 Drawing from her previous experience as a teacher and board-certified counselor, as well as from personal experience, **Tanya J. Peterson, MS, NCC,** writes books and articles that empower people to reduce obstacles like anxiety and move forward to create a quality life. Her books include *The Mindful Path Through Anxiety: An Eight-Week Plan to Quiet Your Mind & Gain Calm*, *101 Ways to Stop Anxiety: Practical Ways to Find Peace; The Mindfulness Workbook for Anxiety: The 8-Week Solution to Help You Manage Anxiety, Worry & Stress; The 5-Minute Anxiety Journal: A Creative Way to Stop Freaking Out; The Mindfulness Journal for Anxiety,* and *Break Free: Acceptance and Commitment Therapy in 3 Steps*. She has written several mental health-themed novels as well. Tanya also writes extensively for the mental health website HealthyPlace.com, including the weekly *Anxiety-Schmanxiety* blog, is a regular contributor to the website ChoosingTherapy.com, and has posts on The Mighty. Connect with her on social media through her website, TanyaJPeterson.com.

CPSIA information can be obtained
at www.ICGtesting.com
Printed in the USA
JSHW011137270121
11242JS00005B/9